A Guide to the Windows of King's College Chapel, Cambridge

MONTAGUE RHODES JAMES

CAMBRIDGE
UNIVERSITY PRESS

CAMBRIDGE UNIVERSITY PRESS

Cambridge, New York, Melbourne, Madrid, Cape Town, Singapore,
São Paolo, Delhi, Dubai, Tokyo

Published in the United States of America by Cambridge University Press, New York

www.cambridge.org
Information on this title: www.cambridge.org/9781108015585

This edition first published 1899
This digitally printed version 2010

ISBN 978-1-108-01558-5 Paperback

A GUIDE

WINDOWS OF
KING'S COLLEGE CHAPEL
CAMBRIDGE

BY

MONTAGUE RHODES JAMES, Litt.D.

FELLOW OF KING'S COLLEGE,
DIRECTOR OF THE FITZWILLIAM MUSEUM.

London:

C. J. CLAY AND SONS,
CAMBRIDGE UNIVERSITY PRESS WAREHOUSE,
AVE MARIA LANE.
1899

Price Sixpence.

A GUIDE

TO THE

WINDOWS OF
KING'S COLLEGE CHAPEL
CAMBRIDGE

BY

MONTAGUE RHODES JAMES, Litt.D.

FELLOW OF KING'S COLLEGE,
DIRECTOR OF THE FITZWILLIAM MUSEUM.

London:
C. J. CLAY AND SONS,
CAMBRIDGE UNIVERSITY PRESS WAREHOUSE,
AVE MARIA LANE.
1899

CAMBRIDGE LIBRARY COLLECTION

Books of enduring scholarly value

Cambridge

The city of Cambridge received its royal charter in 1201, having already been home to Britons, Romans and Anglo-Saxons for many centuries. Cambridge University was founded soon afterwards and celebrated its octocentenary in 2009. This series explores the history and influence of Cambridge as a centre of science, learning, and discovery, its contributions to national and global politics and culture, and its inevitable controversies and scandals.

A Guide to the Windows of King's College Chapel, Cambridge

M. R. James (1862–1936) is probably best remembered as a writer of chilling ghost stories, but he was an outstanding scholar of medieval literature and palaeography, who served both as Provost of King's College, Cambridge, and as Director of the Fitzwilliam Museum, and many of his stories reflect his academic background. His detailed descriptive catalogues of manuscripts owned by colleges, cathedrals and museums are still of value to scholars today. First published in 1899, this book provides a description and brief history of the stained-glass windows in King's College chapel, together with explanations of their symbolism. A description of the remains of painted glass in the side chapels is also included. Now reissued, it will be welcomed by librarians and researchers alike.

Cambridge University Press has long been a pioneer in the reissuing of out-of-print titles from its own backlist, producing digital reprints of books that are still sought after by scholars and students but could not be reprinted economically using traditional technology. The Cambridge Library Collection extends this activity to a wider range of books which are still of importance to researchers and professionals, either for the source material they contain, or as landmarks in the history of their academic discipline.

Drawing from the world-renowned collections in the Cambridge University Library, and guided by the advice of experts in each subject area, Cambridge University Press is using state-of-the-art scanning machines in its own Printing House to capture the content of each book selected for inclusion. The files are processed to give a consistently clear, crisp image, and the books finished to the high quality standard for which the Press is recognised around the world. The latest print-on-demand technology ensures that the books will remain available indefinitely, and that orders for single or multiple copies can quickly be supplied.

The Cambridge Library Collection will bring back to life books of enduring scholarly value (including out-of-copyright works originally issued by other publishers) across a wide range of disciplines in the humanities and social sciences and in science and technology.

PREFACE.

THIS tract is intended for the use of visitors to the Chapel who desire to take something more than a superficial view of the great windows and their subjects. It avoids any critical discussion of the style of the windows, and does not attempt to discriminate the work of the various artists known to have been employed upon them.

A description of the principal remains of the painted glass in the side Chapels is appended.

The best discussions of the style and technique of the glass will be found in a paper by G. Scharf in the *Archaeological Journal* (xiii. 43 sqq.), and in vol. iv. of N. H. J. Westlake's *History of Design in Painted Glass*.

For the history of the windows the *Architectural History of the University of Cambridge*, by Messrs Willis and Clark, vol. i. 498—516 and 581—583 (the latter an Essay by C. J. Evans, M.A., on the Heraldry of the Chapel), is invaluable and indispensable; I have drawn much from it, and have also profited much by the kind help of Mr J. W. Clark, to whom my best thanks are due. For the rest I have relied upon my own examination of the windows.

If this guide proves useful and acceptable, I may be able in a future edition to add some matter of a more critical nature.

MONTAGUE RHODES JAMES.

24 *July,* 1899.

THE glass in the large side-windows and in the east window of King's College Chapel was made and put up between the year 1515 and the year 1531. Three firms were employed to execute it, namely: (1) Barnard Flower, the king's glazier, who died in 1525 or 1526, having by that time completed four windows; (2) Galyon (= Galen) Hoone, Richard Bownde, Thomas Reve, and James Nicholson, all of London; and (3) Francis Williamson and Symon Symondes, also of London. The second and third of these firms are responsible for the east window and twenty out of the twenty-four side windows. It was stipulated that the subjects should represent " the story of the olde lawe and of the new lawe," treated after the model of the windows in King Henry the Seventh's Chapel in Westminster Abbey. Only a single fragmentary figure now remains in the windows of that Chapel.

Each of the side-windows contains:

(1) In the small lights at the top, a number of heraldic devices. These are all by the same hand, and are repeated throughout the Chapel.

(2) In the central light, reaching from top to bottom, four figures of angels and prophets holding inscribed scrolls explanatory of the pictures on either side.

(3) Four pictures, two above and two below the cross-bar or transom; each picture occupies two lights.

The east window contains:

(1) Heraldic devices in the small lights at the top.

(2) Six pictures, each occupying three lights.

As a general rule, the pictures above the cross-bar in the side windows represent scenes from the Old Testament (or elsewhere) typical of those below the bar, which are taken from the New Testament.

The order of the windows is as follows: you begin at the north-west window and go round by the east window to the south-west window, ending with the west window.

Heraldic devices

We will first shortly enumerate the heraldic devices which occur in the tracery lights at the top of the side windows.

They are:

(*a*) In the central light at the top throughout, the arms of Henry VII. encircled with the garter.

(*b*) In the other small lights, the following badges, variously arranged, on shields held by angels:

(1)   The Lancaster Rose (red).
(2)   The Hawthorn Bush.
(3)   The Portcullis.
(4)   The Fleur-de-lys.
(5)   The Tudor Rose (red and white).
(6)   The White Rose in a Sun (for York).
(7)   Initials, H. E. (for Henry VII. and Elizabeth of York).
(8)   Initials, H. R. (= Henricus Rex).
(9)   Initials, H. K. (for Henry VIII. and Katherine of Aragon as Prince and Princess of Wales).

In the east window the heraldic devices differ from these; they will be described when we come to treat of the window.

Subjects and in-scriptions

The main subject of the windows taken as a whole is the Life of the Virgin and the Life of Christ, illustrated by types from the Old Testament and other sources.

The inscriptions are for the most part taken from the Vulgate or Latin translation of the Bible, made by St Jerome. This part of the work has been carelessly executed, and in several of the windows the inscriptions bear no reference to the subjects they are intended to illustrate.

The four pictures in this window are four consecutive scenes relating to the Birth of the Virgin, and not, as usual, types and antitypes. *Window I. at north-west*

Upper Left-hand. A white-bearded Priest in mitre on *L* repels with his hand a white-bearded man, who with his wife goes away sorrowfully to *R*. **A**

This represents the High Priest rejecting the offering of Joachim and Anna, the legendary parents of the Virgin. The story is that Joachim and Anna were good and prosperous, but old and childless; and because they were childless, the priest refused their offering (or made them offer last in order) when they came to the Temple.

Upper Right-hand. The white-bearded man of scene A is kneeling, facing to *R*. Above on *R* is an angel in green and gold, flying downwards. Below the angel are seen a shepherd with bagpipes, a dog, and sheep. **B**

After the rejection of his offering, Joachim retired into the country in sadness. An angel came to him and bade him return to Jerusalem, where he would meet his wife at the Golden Gate of the Temple, and a daughter should be born to them who should be blessed by all generations.

Lower Left-hand. On the *R* is a large portal—the Golden Gate of the Temple: before it Joachim and Anna embrace each other. **C**

Lower Right-hand. On *R* is a bed, blue with red curtains. In it Anna is sitting up. On *L* are various women who have come to see her. In front is the infant Mary (her head is not original) being washed by two women. On a cornice is written SANCTA ANNA MATER MR. (Saint Anne the mother of Mary). **D**

The inscriptions in this window are the same above and below the cross-bar: they are also much broken. They read as follows:

(1) *Post triduum i..unii peperit anna mariam beneuic* (= *benedictam*).

(2) *Angelus in specie iuuenis ap(par)uit ei dicens ut se .... vi decrettus* (?).

(3) *Post ..... ienfrni peperit anna mariam.*

(4) *Angelus in specie iuuenis apparuit.*

The meaning of which is (generally speaking):

(1 and 3)   After three days' fasting (?) Anna brought forth the blessed Mary.

(2 and 4)   An angel in the form of a youth appeared to him, saying......

At the top of this window is the date 1527 twice repeated.

Window II. **A**   *Upper Left-hand.* Men on *L* hold a trestle-table of gold. In the centre is a nude image on an altar holding a banner with a sun on it. On *R* is a priest. Above is an inscription, ALMA REDEMPTORIS MATER, the beginning of a hymn to the Virgin.

The subject of this is the offering of a golden table in the Temple of the Sun. The story was taken by the artist from a medieval collection of types called the *Speculum Humanae Salvationis*, or *Mirror of Man's Salvation*. It is derived from a collection of anecdotes by a Roman writer, Valerius Maximus, who tells the story as follows (*De Dictis Factisque Memorabilibus*, IV. 1. Externa, no. 7):

"Some one had purchased the produce of their next cast from some fishermen who were drawing their nets in the neighbourhood of Miletus. They brought up a great golden Delphic table (or tripod), and a dispute arose: they said they had sold their catch of fish, the other asserted that he had bought whatever the cast might bring up. It was agreed to consult the oracle of Apollo at Delphi on the point, and the answer was:

"'He who is first of all men in wisdom, to him let the tripod be given.' So they offered it to Thales of Miletus.

He in modesty yielded it to Bias of Priene, and he to Pittacus: and thus it went the round of the Seven Wise Men of Greece till it reached Solon of Athens, who, judging the god to be the wisest, offered the prize to Apollo."

This offering of the pure gold table in the temple of Apollo was taken in the middle ages to be a type of the presentation of the pure Virgin in the temple of God, which is represented below.

Underneath the picture are two small half-length figures holding scrolls referring to other types of the same thing. Similar figures do not occur in any of the other windows.

The first has the words *Hester iii°*, referring to the presentation of Esther to Ahasuerus.

The second: *Yepte obtulit filiam suam domino,* "Jephthah offered his daughter to the Lord," which was also considered a type of the presentation of the Virgin.

Lower Left-hand. Presentation of the Virgin. She is　B
seen as a young girl in blue, walking up the steps of the altar, at the top of which stands the priest. Her parents are below. The story is that when the Virgin was three years old her parents brought her to the temple, where she walked up the fifteen steps of the altar of her own accord. Thenceforth she lived in the temple, and was fed by angels.

Below this picture are half-length figures with scrolls, of which only one is legible: *Primo libro Regum iii* (i.e. 1 Kings iii.), referring to the presentation of Samuel in the Temple in 1 Sam. (1 Kings) ii., iii.

Upper Right-hand. A marriage scene; an angel on *R.*　C
It is the marriage of Tobias with Sara (Tobit vii. 13). The angel is the angel Raphael, who accompanied Tobias in the form of a man.

On a pillar is written BENEDICTVS SIT DOMINVS.

Only one scroll of those held by the small figures below is legible. It reads: *Regina persarum[1] contemplabatur,* "The

---

[1] Written 'ysarum.'

queen of the Persians looked." This is a reference to the
Speculum Humanae Salvationis mentioned above. In it we
find the story of the King of Persia and the hanging gardens
he constructed for his wife used as a type of the presentation
of the Virgin, or rather, of her seclusion in the temple.

D   *Lower Right-hand.* The marriage of Mary and Joseph.
Joseph holds a rod.

The story is that when the Virgin grew up, the High
Priest was told by an angel to send for all the unmarried
men in Israel: each man was to bring a rod with him, and
he in whose rod a sign was seen should be the husband of
the Virgin. Joseph, though an old man, had to come with
the rest; and a dove flew out of his rod and perched upon
his head.

Inscriptions, from the top.

(1)   Referring to C:
Hic Sara desponsatur Thobie m(inori).
Here Sara is espoused to Tobias the younger.

(2)   Referring to A:
Mensa aurea   *oblata est in templo.*
The golden table   was offered in the temple.

(3)   Referring to B:
Maria domino oblata est in templo.
Mary was offered to the Lord in the temple.

(4)   Referring to D:
Hic Virgo Maria desponsatur Ioseph.
Here the Virgin Mary is espoused to Joseph.

Below the second "messenger" (as the scroll-bearing
figures are called) is a half-length figure of the Child Christ
with orb and inscription: *Ego sum alpha*, etc., I am Alpha
and Omega.

The lowest messenger has on his girdle the words FELIX
NAMQVE, the beginning of an antiphon to the Virgin.

Upper Left-hand. The Temptation of Eve. She stands by the tree and takes the apple from the serpent, which, as usual in medieval pictures, has a human head and arms.

This is rather a contrast to, than a type of, the subject below, which is the Annunciation.

The inscription (uppermost in the central light) is:

> *precepit deus no(bis ne comede)remus et ne tangeremus illud.*

> God commanded us that we should not eat nor touch it. (Gen. iii. 3.)

Lower Left-hand. The Annunciation: Gabriel on the **B** left, attended by smaller angels; the Dove flying towards the head of the Virgin. On a cornice is written *Ecce ancilla domini.*

The inscription, third in the central light, is:

> *en* (for *et tu*) *bethleem terra iude non eris minima inter prin(cipes).*

> lo, Bethlehem (in the) land of Judah, thou shalt not be the least among the princes. (Matt. ii. 6.)

Upper Right-hand. On *L* the burning bush with God **C** in it. On *R* Moses takes off his shoe. Sheep and dog in the middle distance. In the background on *R* Moses is seen departing with his rod. A type of the Nativity because, as the bush was not consumed, so Mary remained a virgin after the birth of Christ.

Inscription (second in central light):

> *(App)aruit (ei Dominu)s in flamma ignis de medio ru(bi).*

> The Lord appeared unto him in a flame of fire from the midst of a bush. (Exod. iii. 2.)

Lower Right-hand. The Nativity. Joseph, Mary, and **D** a number of little angels adore the Child. Through an opening in the background is seen the angel appearing to the shepherds.

Inscription (lowest in the central light):

> *Natus est Ihesus in bethleem iude regnante herode.*
> *Ma. ii.*

> Jesus was born in Bethlehem of Judaea in the reign
> of Herod.   Matt. ii. (1).

Window IV. **A**   *Upper Left-hand.*   The Circumcision of Isaac, by Abraham.

Inscription (uppermost):

> *vocavitque Abraham nomen filii sui Isaac et circum-*
> *cidit eum octavo die.*

> and Abraham called the name of his son Isaac, and
> circumcised him the eighth day.   (Gen. xxi. 3,
> 4.)

B   *Lower Left-hand.*   The Circumcision of Christ.

Inscription (third):

> *Impleti sunt dies octo ut aranderetur* (for *circumci-*
> *deretur*) *puer.   Luce 2.*

> Eight days were fulfilled for the circumcising of the
> child.   Luke ii. (21).

C   *Upper Right-hand.*   The Queen of Sheba (on *R*) visiting
Solomon (throned on *L*).

Inscription (second):

> *dedit regi centum et viginti ta(lenta) auri et aromata*
> *multa.   3 regum.*

> She gave the king an hundred and twenty talents of
> gold, and much spices.   3 Kings.   (1 Kings x. 10.)

D   *Lower Right-hand.*   The Adoration of the Magi.   The
Virgin and Child on *R.*: the star above.

Inscription (lowest):

> *procidentes adorauerunt eum (et) apertis thesauris suis*
> *obtulerunt ei munera.*

> They fell down and worshipped him (and) opened their
> treasures and offered him gifts.   (Matt. ii. 11.)

Upper Left-hand. The Purification of Women under the Window
V. **A**
Law. The scene is the Temple; and a woman is offering
doves according to the ordinance. At top on *L* is a figure
of Moses. On the altar-cloth are the letters RICAH (?).

Inscription (uppermost) not easily legible. It begins:

Sancti(fica) mi(hi) omne primogenitum quod aperu...

Sanctify unto me every firstborn that openeth (the
womb). (Exod. xiii. 2.)

Lower Left-hand. The Presentation of Christ in the   **B**
Temple. Simeon is a conspicuous figure.

Inscription (third):

*Adduxerunt(?) illum in Hierusalem ut sisterent eum
domino ut scriptum est in lege domini.*

They brought him to Jerusalem to present him unto
the Lord, as it is written in the law of the Lord.
(Luke ii. 22, 23.)

Upper Right-hand. Jacob, a yellow-haired youth, saying   **C**
farewell to Isaac (seated, with turban) before he flees from
Esau. In the background on *R* Rebecca is seen bringing
him to Isaac to be blessed. Further off on *L* he is seen
again, perhaps wrestling with the angel.

Inscription (second) mostly gone:

Ecce Esau frater tuus min[atur ut] occ(id)at te.

Lo, Esau thy brother threateneth to kill thee. (Gen.
xxvii. 42.)

Lower Right-hand. The Flight into Egypt. An idol   **D**
falling from a pillar on the right of the mullion[1]. In the
background is seen a cornfield, a husbandman, and soldiers.
This refers to the popular legend (which occurs in no
apocryphal gospel, but appears in Christmas Carols, as well
as in medieval works of art) that the Holy Family in their
flight passed a man sowing corn. They said to him: " If
any one should come this way and enquire for us, tell them

[1] See below, Window VI. **B.**

that we passed by when you were sowing your seed." The corn immediately sprang up and ripened, and when Herod's soldiers came and enquired after the Child and His mother, the husbandman was reaping his crop. Then, as the carol of *The Carnal and the Crane*[1] says:

> "Turn back," says the captain,
> "Your labour and mine's in vain:
>   It's full three-quarters of a year
>   Since he has his seed sown."

Inscription (lowest):

> *Surge et accipite (puerum et matrem) eius et fuge in Egyptum et esto ibi usque.*

> Rise and take the young Child and His mother and flee into Egypt and be there until.... (Matt. ii. 13.)

Window VI. **A**   *Upper Left-hand.* The golden calf, conspicuous on a ruby pillar. Moses has cast down and broken the tables on which, as often in medieval pictures, seems to be inscribed the beginning of the Apostles' Creed.

Inscription (second):

> *Iratusque valde proiecit de manu tabulas et confregit eas.*

> And he was very wroth and cast the tables out of his hand and brake them. (Ex. xxxii. 19.)

B   *The Idols of Egypt falling.* The scene is a temple. The Virgin (crowned) carrying the child, is on *L.* Two idols are falling from their pillars in the centre. On *R* a kneeling figure in a rich dress; this is Aphrodosius, the governor of the city, who adored the Virgin and Child (*Gospel of Pseudo-Matthew* or *Liber de infantia*, cap. xxiv.). At the bottom are the figures 15017, generally read as a date (1517). Note that on Aphrodosius' shoulder is a band with lettering ROBOAM AVTEM GENVIT.

---

[1] Printed in Sylvester's *Christmas Carols*, etc. A "Carnal" means a young Crane.

Inscription (third) almost illegible:

> *Dominus ascendet super nubem levem et ingredietur*
> *(Egyptum et commovebuntur simulacra Egypti a*
> *facie eius). Es.*

> The Lord shall ride upon a light cloud and shall come
> into Egypt, and the idols of Egypt shall be moved
> at his presence. Isa. (xix. 1).

Upper Right-hand. The Massacre of the seed royal by   **C**
Athaliah. Athaliah (a figure like that of the Virgin) and a
ruler in red stand above. The massacre is going on below.

Inscription (uppermost) illegible.

Lower Right-hand. The Massacre of the Innocents.   **D**
Herod on horseback is seen on *L*.

Inscription (lowest):

> *Et missis satellitibus (interfecit) omnes pueros (qui erant*
> *in Bethleem). Mat. 2°.*

> And he sent messengers and slew all the children that
> were in Bethlehem. Matt. ii. (16).

Upper Left-hand. Naaman washing himself in Jordan, Window
a servant on the bank : horses etc. in the background.   VII. **A**

Inscription (second):

> *Naaman leprosus sepcies (lavit) et mundatus est.*
> Naaman the leper washed seven times and was cleansed.
> (2 Kings v. 14.)

Lower Left-hand. The Baptism of Christ. The Father   **B**
at the top, half-length : the Dove below Him. Three angels
hold the clothes of Christ. A fourth angel above on *R*, and
an angel and lamb in the background.

Inscription (third):

> *Baptizatus autem Ihesus confestim ascendit de aqua et*
> *aperti sunt ei celi et vidit.*

> Now Jesus when He was baptized went up straightway
> out of the water, and the heavens were opened
> unto Him and He saw .... (Matt. iii. 16.)

C   *Upper Right-hand.* Jacob tempts Esau to sell his birthright. Jacob is seated at a table on *R,* eating. Esau enters hastily from *L* with dogs.

Inscription (uppermost):

Ait Iacob Iura ergo mihi. Juravit ei Esau et vendidit. Jacob saith: Swear thou unto me. Esau sware unto him and sold (the birthright). (Gen. xxv. 33.)

D   *Lower Right-hand.* The Temptation of Christ. Below in front the devil (represented as an old man) tempts Christ to turn stones into bread. Above on *L* the two are seen on the high mountain: on *R* they stand on the pinnacle of the temple.

Inscription (lowest):

Et accedens tentator dixit ei si filius dei (es) dic ut (lapi)des isti pa(nes fiant).

And the tempter came and said to Him: If thou be the Son of God, command that these stones be made bread. (Matt. iv. 3.)

*** The following windows were releaded by Hedgeland (1845—1849) and much new glass inserted. The heads put in by him are conspicuously bad.

Window VIII. A   *Upper Left-hand.* Elisha raises the Shunammite's son. Note the house-front, with a shelf and dishes standing on it.

Inscription (second):

Tolle filium tuum uenit illa et corruit ad pedes eius et adorauit super terram tulit filium suum et egressa est. regum.

Take up thy son. And she came and fell at his feet and adored on the earth (and) took up her son and went out. (4) Kings (iv. 36).

B   *Lower Left-hand.* The Raising of Lazarus. Nearly all the heads are Hedgeland's.

Inscription (lowest):

> *Lazare veni foras et prodiit qui fuerat mortuus.*
> *Joannis* 11.

> Lazarus, come forth. And he that was dead came
> forth. John xi. (43, 44).

Upper Right-hand. The Triumph of David. David **C**
enters on *L* balancing the huge head of Goliath on the
point of a sword. On *R* are the women with musical
instruments.

Inscription (uppermost):

> *Assumens autem Dauid caput Philisthaei attulit illud*
> *in Ierusalem.*

> And David took the head of the Philistine and brought
> it to Jerusalem. (1 Sam. xvii. 54.)

Lower Right-hand. The Entry into Jerusalem. A man **D**
in a tree cuts down branches: others spread garments.
Many bad new heads by Hedgeland.

Inscription (third):

> *Ecce rex tuus venit mansuetus sedens super asinam.*

> Behold, thy King cometh, meek, sitting upon an ass.
(John xii. 15.)

Upper Left-hand. The Fall of the Manna. Moses with Window
rod conspicuous on *L*. The Manna is falling in the form of IX. **A**
white discs.

Inscription (second):

> *Panem de celo praestiti(sti) eis sapiencie* 16.

> Thou didst give them bread from heaven. Wisdom
> xvi. (20).

Lower Left-hand. The Last Supper. Christ on *L* **B**
stands and gives the sop to Judas, who bends over the table
from *R*. He is red-haired.

Inscription (third):

Desiderio desideravi hoc pascha comedere vobiscum antequam patior. Luce 22.

With desire have I desired to eat this passover with you before I suffer.   Luke xxii. (15).

C   *Upper Right-hand.*   The Fall of the angels.   At top on *L* the Father is seen throned.   On *R* the angels who did not fall are praising Him.   Below His feet Michael thrusts down the fallen angels, who become more monstrous in form as they approach the bottom.

This subject is chosen to pair with the Agony in the Garden below because in John xii. 31, xvi. 11, just before the Passion Christ speaks of the "casting out" and "judging" of the prince of this world.

Inscription (uppermost):

Si ceciderint in terram a semetipsis non resurgent.

If they fall upon the earth they will not rise again of themselves.   Baruch vi. (Epistle of Jeremy) 27.

D   *Lower Right-hand.*   The Agony in the Garden.   Note the smaller scale of the figures, the roundness of the heads, and the nimbi given to Christ and the Apostles.   Another artist has been at work in some of the scenes here.

Inscription (lowest):

Pater si vis transfer. Luce 22.

Father, if it be Thy will, remove.   Luke xxii. (42).

Window   *Upper Left-hand.*   Cain and Abel.   In the foreground
X. A   Cain kills Abel with a jawbone: behind their sacrifice is seen.   The fire of Abel's altar goes up straight towards the figure of God in the sky, who accepts it: that of Cain's altar sweeps along the ground on *R.*

Inscription (second):

Consurrexit Cain adversus fratrem suum. Gen. 4°.

Cain rose up against his brother.   Gen. iv. (8).

Lower Left-hand.   The Betrayal.   Judas kisses Christ: B
Peter attacks Malchus.

Inscription (third):

> *Dixit ave Rabbi et osculatus est eum.*
>
> He said: Hail, Master! and kissed Him. (Matt. xxvi. 49.)

Upper Right-hand.   Shimei (on *L*) cursing David.   C

Inscription (uppermost):

> *Egredere egredere vir sanguinum et vir belial.   2 regum*
> *16.*
>
> Come out, come out, thou bloody man and thou man
> of Belial.   2 Kings (Sam.) xvi. 7.

Lower Right-hand.   Christ mocked and blindfolded.   D
Annas and other Jews look on from above.

Inscription (lowest):

> *Velaverunt eum et percutiebant faciem eius.   Lu.* 22.
>
> They blindfolded Him, and smote His face.   Luke
> xxii. (64).

Upper Left-hand.   Jeremiah imprisoned.   The princes Window
are locking the door of a tower on *L*.   XI.   A

Inscription (second):

> *Irati principes contra Jeremiam cesum eum miserunt in*
> *carcerem.   Ihe.* 37.
>
> The princes were wroth with Jeremiah, and smote him,
> and put him in prison.   Jer. xxxvii. (15).

Lower Left-hand.   Christ before Annas.   On the throne   B
on *R* is written: SIC RESPONDES PONTIFICI (Answerest thou
the high-priest so?   John xviii. 22).

Inscription (third):

> *Johannes ca* XVIII.   *Si male locutus sum testimonium*
> *perhibe de malo.*
>
> John xviii. (23).   If I have spoken evil, bear witness of
> the evil.

C   *Upper Right-hand.* The Shame of Noah. Ham in the background on *R* mocks him.

Inscription (uppermost):

> *Bibensque noe vinum inebriatus est et nudatus. Genesi.*
>
> And Noah drank wine, and was drunken, and was uncovered. Gen. (ix. 21).

D   *Lower Right-hand.* Christ before Herod.

Inscription (lowest):

> *Ve qui dicitis malum bonum et bonum malum. Ysaie v.*
>
> Woe unto you that call evil good, and good evil. Isa. v. (20).

Window XII. A   *Upper Left-hand.* Job tormented. He sits on the dung-hill. Two magnificent devils are scourging him. A third is in the air. On *R* stands his wife mocking him.

Inscription (second):

> *Dominus dedit abstulit dominus sit nomen domini benedictum.*
>
> The Lord gave, the Lord hath taken away: blessed be the name of the Lord. (Job i. 21.)

B   *Lower Left-hand.* The Scourging of Christ. Note the face of Christ, which seems to be purposely made unpleasing: "There is no beauty in Him that we should desire Him."

Inscription (third):

> *Tunc ergo apprehendit pilatus Ihesum et flagellauit eum.* S. JOANNEM 19.
>
> Then Pilate therefore took Jesus and scourged Him. John xix. 1.

C   *Upper Right-hand.* Solomon crowned on *R*. The daughters of Zion coming to behold him.

Inscription (uppermost):

> *Egredimini et videte filie sion regem Salomonem.*
> *Cant.*

> Go forth, O ye daughters of Zion, and behold king
> Solomon (with the crown wherewith his mother
> crowned him in the day of his espousals). Can-
> ticles (iii. 11).

Lower Right-hand. Christ crowned with thorns. **D**

Inscription (lowest).

> *Et milites plectentes coronam de spinis imposuerunt*
> *capiti eius.*

> And the soldiers platted a crown of thorns, and put it
> on his head. (John xix. 2.)

The East Window. XIII.
The East
In the tracery lights we have : Window

In the centre the arms of Henry VII. on a banner held
by a red dragon. In the side lights the Lancaster Rose (red),
the Tudor Rose (red and white), the Ostrich Feather with
scroll *Ich dien,* the Fleur de lys, the Portcullis, and the
initials H. R., H. E., and H. K. The pictures are six in
number, each occupying three lights.

Lower Left-hand. Ecce homo. Christ shewn to the people **A**
by Pilate, with the words : Behold the man !

Lower Centre. Pilate washing his hands. Christ is before **B**
him, back to the spectator.

Lower Right-hand. Christ bearing the Cross. A spiked **C**
table of wood attached to His girdle. Towards *L* Veronica
kneels, offering Him the kerchief on which according to legend
He wiped His face, and impressed His likeness upon it.
The red patch in the upper *R* corner represents a piece of
ground, possibly the Field of Blood, as has been suggested.

Upper Left-hand. Christ nailed to the Cross. **D**

E   *Upper Centre.* Christ crucified with the Thieves. On *L* the soldier pierces His side. On *R* are the Virgin and John. Mary Magdalene embraces the Cross. In front are the soldiers casting lots; and behind on *R* the Centurion with a scroll : *Vere filius dei erat iste* (Truly this was the Son of God. Matt. xxvii. 54).

F   *Upper Right-hand.* Christ taken down from the Cross.

This window was not touched by Hedgeland. The following six, however, were restored by him.

The South-East Window.

Window XIV. at south-east   There was originally only half a window here. The lower half was intended to have a building (which was in part begun) abutting on it. This building was removed in 1827 and the lower part of the window opened up. The old glass was moved down to the lower lights in 1841 : and in 1845 the glass which now occupies the upper main lights was inserted by Hedgeland.

In the lower half of the window the type and antitype are placed side by side.

A   *Upper half* The Brazen Serpent : after a picture by Rubens, now in the National Gallery. A type of the Crucifixion. Glass by Hedgeland, of which it would be difficult to exaggerate the badness.

B   *Lower Left-hand.* Naomi and her daughters-in-law lamenting over her husband Elimelech. In the background Naomi, Ruth, and Orpah are seen.

Inscription (lowest) :

Ne uocetis me Noemi. Ruth primo capitulo.

Call me not Naomi. Ruth i. (20).

C   *Lower Right-hand.* The Virgin and the other holy women lamenting over the body of Christ.

Inscription (uppermost):

> *Quin et tuam ipsius animam penetrabit gladius. Luce 2 capitulo.*
>
> Yea, and a sword shall pierce through thine own heart also. Luke ii. (35).

Upper Left-hand. Joseph cast into the pit by his brothers. Window XV. **A**

Inscription (uppermost):

> *Et mittamus eum in cisternam veterem que est in solitudine. Genes. 37.*
>
> And let us put him into (this) old pit which is in the wilderness. Gen. xxxvii. (22).

Lower Left-hand. The Burial of Christ. Note the crown **B** of thorns in front.

Inscription (lowest):

> *Posuit illud in monumento suo nouo. Mathe. 27°.*
>
> He put it in his own new tomb. Matt. xxvii. (60).

Upper Right-hand. Israel going out of Egypt. **C**

Inscription (second):

> *Eduxit Ysrahel de egipto per turmas suas. exodi 12°.*
>
> He brought Israel out of Egypt by their companies. Ex. xii. (51).

Lower Right-hand. The Harrowing of Hell. Christ **D** stands on the Devil and the broken gates of Hell. The souls of Adam and Eve and the ancient Fathers adore Him. There are admirable demons above.

Inscription (third):

> *Aduenisti desideratus saluator mundi. Augustinus.*
>
> Thou art come the desired one, the Saviour of the world. Augustine.

From a spurious sermon of Augustine quoted in the *Legenda Aurea* (liv. de Resurrectione Domini).

Window XVI. **A**   *Upper Left-hand.* Jonah vomited up by the fish. Nineveh in the distance.

Inscription (second):

Evomuit Jonam in aridam. Jhone 2°.

It vomited up Jonah on the dry land. Jonah ii. (11).

B   *Lower Left-hand.* The Resurrection of Christ.

Inscription (third):

Revolvit lapidem et sedebat super eum. Matt. 28.

He rolled away the stone and sat upon it. Matt. xxviii. (2).

C   *Upper Right-hand.* Anna, the mother of Tobias, who had given her son up for dead, sees him return accompanied by Azarias (the angel Raphael in disguise) and his dog. Their suite is seen in the background.

Inscription (uppermost):

Et illico cognovit venientem filium suum. Tobie ca.

And immediately she recognised her son coming. Tobit (xi. 6).

D   *Lower Right-hand.* Christ appearing to His Mother at prayer. The incident is not narrated in the apocryphal Gospels, but is assumed by St Ambrose, and discussed in the *Legenda Aurea* (liv. de Resurrectione Domini).

Inscription (lowest):

Salve sancta parens enixa est puerpera regem qui celum terramque regit.

Hail holy mother, the woman in travail hath borne a king who ruleth heaven and earth.

From a hymn to the Virgin. The word *est* is intruded wrongly, spoiling the hexameter.

Window XVII. **A**   *Upper Left-hand.* Reuben at the pit finds it empty and Joseph gone.

Inscription (second):

> (*Reversus*) *que ruben ad cisternam non invenit puerum.*
> *Ge.* 37.
>
> And Reuben returning to the pit found not the lad.
> Gen. xxxvii. 29.

Lower Left-hand.   The three Marys with spices come to   **B**
the sepulchre and find it empty.

Inscription (third):

> *Et valde mane primo die Sab(bati) veniunt ad monu-*
> *mentum exorto sole.   Mar.* 16.
>
> And very early in the morning on the first day of the
> week they came to the sepulchre when the sun
> was up.   Mark xvi. (2).

Upper Right-hand.   Darius visiting the lions' den finds   **C**
Daniel alive.   One of the lions is very oddly drawn.

Inscription (uppermost):

> *Venit autem rex die [septima et clamavit voce] ingenti*
> *Daniele, Daniele.*
>
> But the king came on the seventh day and cried with
> a loud voice: Daniel, Daniel.   Cf. Bel and the
> Dragon = Dan. xiv. 40, 41.

Lower Right-hand.   Christ, with spade, appears to Mary   **D**
Magdalene in the garden.   The introduction of the spade,
common in later art, is extremely unintelligent.   Mary
Magdalene is seen alone in the background, looking into
the sepulchre.

Inscription (lowest):

> *Hec cum dixit, conuersa est retrorsum et vidit Iesum*
> *stantem.   Joh. xx.*
>
> When she had said this, she turned about and saw
> Jesus standing.   Joh. xx. (16).

The inscriptions in this window are all wrongly inserted.
They refer to subjects in the Acts of the Apostles which
occur in window XXI., and are repeated in their proper
place.   I give them below.

A *Upper Left-hand.* The angel Raphael disguised as a young man meets Tobias and offers to accompany him on his journey. (Tobit v. 4.)

B *Lower Left-hand.* Christ disguised as a wayfarer meets the two disciples going to Emmaus.

C *Upper Right-hand.* The prophet Habakkuk is caught up by an angel when going to feed the reapers in the field, and is carried to Babylon to feed Daniel in the lions' den. (Bel and the Dragon = Dan. xiv. 33 sqq.)

D *Lower Right-hand.* The Supper at Emmaus. Christ is known to the disciples in breaking of bread. Note that the bread He has broken is divided evenly as if by a knife. In the Coventry plays (*Emmaus*) Lucas says:

> He brak the lof as evyn on tway
> > as ony sharpe knyff xuld kytt breed (should cut bread)
> Therby we knew the trewthe that day
> > that Cryst dede live and was not deed.

The inscriptions are

1. Uppermost :

    Et dimiserunt eos. illi quidem ibant gaudentes a conspectu concilii. Actuum 5°.

    And they sent them away. And they departed rejoicing from before the council. Acts v. (40, 41).

2. Second :

    Petrus autem dixit Argentum et aurum non est mihi quod autem habeo. 3. Ca.

    But Peter said, Silver and gold have I none ; but that which I have (give I thee). Acts iii. (6).

3. *Quomodo utique convenit vobis tentare spiritum[Quid] domini. Act. v.*

    How have ye conspired to tempt the Spirit of the Lord ? Acts v. (9).

4. *Viri iudei et qui habitatis Ierusalem universi hoc vobis notum sit. Act. 2°.*

Men of Judæa, and all ye that live at Jerusalem, be
this known unto you. Acts ii. (14).

This is the last of the windows that were repaired by
Hedgeland.

Upper Left-hand. The Prodigal Son returns, and is
embraced by his father.

Window
XIX. **A**

Inscription (uppermost):

Pater peccavi in celum et coram te.   Luce 15 ca°.

Father, I have sinned against heaven and before thee.
Luke xv. (24).

Lower Left-hand. The Incredulity of St Thomas.   **B**

Inscription (third):

*Pax vobiscum deinde dixit thome infer digitum tuum
huc et vide manus meas.   Iohan. 20. ca°.*

Peace be unto you. Then saith he to Thomas, Reach
hither thy finger, and behold my hands. Joh.
xx. (27).

Upper Right-hand. The Meeting of Jacob and Joseph   **C**
in Egypt.

Inscription (second):

*Dixit iacop ad ioseph iam letus moriar quia vidi faciem
tuam.   Ge. 46. ca°.*

Jacob said unto Joseph, Now shall I die happy, since I
have seen thy face. Gen. xlvi. (30).

Lower Right-hand. Christ appearing to the Apostles   **D**
without Thomas.

Inscription (lowest):

*Pax vobiscum.   et cum hoc dixisset ostendit eis manus
et latus.   Johan. 20. ca°.*

Peace be unto you. And when He had so said, He
shewed unto them His hands and His side. Joh.
xx. (20).

This subject and its type (C, D) ought to precede the
other (A, B).

Upper Left-hand. The Translation of Elijah in a car drawn by horses. He casts his mantle down to Elisha.

Inscription (*third* : it should be second):

Cumque transissent helias (dixit) ad heliseum. 3 regum 2° ca°.

And when they had passed over, Elijah said to Elisha. 3 (2) Kings ii. (9).

B   *Lower Left-hand.* The Ascension. The Virgin and Apostles surrounding the mount.

Inscription (lowest):

Quis est iste qui venit de Edom tinctis vestibus. Esaie 63.

Who is this that cometh from Edom with dyed garments ? Isa. lxiii. (1).

C   *Upper Right-hand.* Moses on Sinai receiving the tables of the Law from God's hand. The people below the mount.

Note that this subject comes exactly opposite that of the golden calf on the north side.

Inscription (uppermost):

Videns autem populus quod moram faceret moyses. Exod. 32° capit°.

And when the people saw that Moses delayed. Exod. xxxii. (1).

D   *Lower Right-hand.* The Descent of the Holy Ghost upon the Apostles. The Virgin seated in the midst.

Inscription (*second* : should be third):

Spiritus domini replevit orbem terrarum. Sa. (pri)mo.

The spirit of the Lord hath filled the world. Wisdom i. (7).

On the messenger's arm is a band of lettering 1° HENR. and there are many other patches of extraneous glass in the window.

This and the two following windows contain a series of subjects from the Acts of the Apostles, without illustrative types. Subjects from this book are of very rare occurrence in early medieval art. Their presence here has seemed to me to be not unconnected with the revival of interest in that book which marked the Reformation period. Two of the pictures show the influence of Raphael's famous cartoons. In this and the next window figures of St Luke, habited as a doctor with his ox by him, alternate with figures of angels in the central light.

Upper Left-hand.   Peter and the Apostles going to the   **A**
Temple. In the background, Peter preaching inside a building.

Inscription (*third :* should be uppermost) :

> *Viri iudei et qui habitatis Iherusalem uniuersi hoc*
> *vobis notum sit.   Actu. 2° ca°.*

See above, window XVIII. no. 4.

Lower Left-hand.   Peter and John heal the lame man   **B**
(on *L.*) at the gate of the Temple.

Inscription (lowest):

> *Petrus autem dixit, Argentum et aurum non est michi*
> *quod autem habeo (hoc tibi do. Act.) 3° ca°.*

See above, XVIII. no. 2.

Lower Right-hand.   The Death of Ananias.   He lies in   **C**
front before some steps on which stand the Apostles.   In the background is seen his body being carried out for burial.

The design of this picture is copied from Raphael's cartoon.

Inscription wanting.   The proper text is in window XVIII. no. 3.   Instead of it we have in the uppermost place, a text with no picture to refer to :

> *Et dimiserunt eos (et) illi quidem (iban)t gaudentes a*
> *conspectu concilii.   Actuum 5° ca°.*

See above, XVIII. no. 1.

Upper Right-hand.   The Apostles, arrested, are led out   **D**
of a gate on *L.*   In the background, Peter and John are seen bound to a pillar and scourged.

Inscription (second):

(for *adveniens*)   (for *princeps*)   (*et omnes*)
*Advenientes autem principes sacerdotum......qui cum eo
erant conuocauerunt concilium.   Act. 5°.*

But the chief of the priests and all that were with him
coming assembled a council.   Acts v. (21).

Window
XXII. **A**   *Upper Left-hand.* The Conversion of St Paul.   Christ
above.

Inscription (uppermost):

*Et subito circum fulsit eum lux de celo et cadens in
terram audivit vocem dicentem Saule quare per(se-
queris me).*

And suddenly there shined round him a light from
heaven : and he fell to the earth, and heard a voice
saying, Saul, why persecutest thou me ? (Acts ix.
3, 4.)

B   *Upper Right-hand.*   Paul conversing with Jews or
disciples at Damascus.   In the background he is seen being
let down in a basket from a window.

Inscription (second):

*Fuit autem Saulus cum discipulis qui erant Damasci
dies aliquot.*

But Saul was with the disciples that were at Damascus
certain days.   Acts ix. 19.

C   *Lower Left-hand.*   Paul and Barnabas at Lystra.   The
priest brings oxen to sacrifice to them.   Modified from
Raphael's cartoon.

Inscription (lowest):

*Sacerdos autem Jovis qui erat ante ciuitatem illorum
tauros et coronas ad vestibulos.   Act. 14.*

But the priest of Jupiter, that was before their city,
(brought) oxen and garlands to the gates.   Acts
xiv. (13).

Lower Right-hand.   Paul stoned by a crowd of Jews at   **D**
Lystra.

Inscription (third):

> *Superuenerunt autem quidam ab anti(o)chia et iconio
> iudei qui cum persuasissent......paulum. Act.* 14.

> But there came certain Jews from Antioch and
> Iconium, who, when they had persuaded (the
> multitude, stoned) Paul.   Acts xiv. (18).

Lower Left-hand.   Paul saying farewell at Philippi.   Note Window
the ship in the background.   Were it not for the text, one XXIII. **A**
would be inclined to call this scene Paul's farewell to Miletus.

Inscription (third):

> *Cum soluissemus igitur a Troade recto cursu venimus
> Samothracen.*

> When therefore we had loosed from Troas, we came with
> a straight course to Samothrace.   (Acts xvi. 11.)

Upper Left-hand.   Paul at Philippi exorcises the woman   **B**
with the spirit of divination.

Inscription (second):

> *Precipio tibi in nomine Iesu Christi exire ab ea.   Act.*

> I command thee, in the name of Jesus Christ, to come
> out of her.   Acts (xvi. 18).

Upper Right-hand.   Paul brought before the chief captain   **C**
Lysias at Jerusalem.

Inscription (uppermost):

> *Et apprehendentes paulum trahebant eum extra
> templum.   Act.*

> And they caught hold on Paul and drew him out of
> the temple.   Acts (xxi. 30).

Lower Right-hand.   Paul before Nero.   Note the imperial   **D**
crown of the latter.

Inscription (lowest):

> ?
> *permissum est paulo permanere sibimet cum custodiente*
> *se milite.   Act. 28.*

Paul was suffered to dwell by himself with the soldier
that kept him.   Acts xxviii. (16).

Window XXIV.   We here return to the series of type and antitype.   The
last two windows illustrate the death, assumption and glori-
fication of the Virgin, just as the two immediately opposite
illustrate her birth and infancy.

The lower half of the window has suffered much from
accidental breakage.

A   *Upper Left-hand.*   The death of Tobit.   His son Tobias,
the angel Raphael, and the wives of Tobit and Tobias are
round the bed.

Inscription (second):

> *In hora mortis vocavit filium suum cum aliis* (?).

In the hour of his death he called his son with others.
(Tobit xiv. 3.)

B   *Lower Left-hand.*   The Death of the Virgin.   She is
habited in blue and lies in bed.   St John on *R* is placing
a lighted candle in her hands.   St Peter bends over her with
a holy water sprinkler.   The other Apostles, one with a
cross, another with a book, are grouped round.   Through an
opening high up on *L* is seen a half-length figure of God
the Father in the air.

Inscription (lowest), duplicate of that to scene **A**:

> *In hora mortis vocauit filium......thobie.*

C   *Upper Right-hand.*   The Burial of Jacob.   The patri-
archs are following the coffin in black cloaks and hoods.

Inscription (uppermost):

> *Iosep* (*cum*) *fratribus sepeliuit iacop.   Genesis.*

Joseph with his brethren buried Jacob.   Gen. (l. 7) etc.

Lower Right-hand. The Funeral of the Virgin. The   **D**
apostles are carrying the coffin (with white pall and gold
cross). To *R* one carries a palm branch (which had been
brought to the Virgin by an angel in sign of her approaching
death). Below in front are two figures on the ground. Each
is deprived of one hand, which hand is clinging to the pall
of the Virgin's coffin. The story is that the Jews attacked
the procession, and one (or two) of the foremost tried to
upset the bier. Their hands were struck off miraculously
and clung to it: then they repented, and were healed by
Peter. The legend is told in many forms, notably in one
ascribed to Melito, Bishop of Sardis, and embodied in the
Legenda aurea.

Inscription (third) a duplicate of that to scene C:

> *Iosep (cum) fratribus sepeliuit iacop...*

Upper Left-hand. The Translation of Enoch. Enoch, Window
an aged man in a cope, is borne up by angels towards the XXV. **A**
Father, who is above on *L*. Landscape below.

Inscription (uppermost) erased, probably by Hedgeland.
It was a duplicate of that in window XIV., scene C.

> *Eduxit dominus ystrahel de terra egipti.*
> The Lord brought Israel out of Egypt.

Lower Left-hand. The Assumption of the Virgin. She   **B**
is surrounded by angels, some with musical instruments.
A landscape below. The original head of the Virgin is gone.

Inscription (third): modern. Inserted in 1898 in place
of a blank coloured scroll which Hedgeland had quite in-
excusably put in. The work was done by Mr J. E. Kempe.

> *Assumpta est virgo maria in celum, gaudent angeli,*
> *letantur archangeli.*

> The Virgin Mary hath been taken up into heaven.
> Angels are glad, archangels rejoice. (From the
> Roman Breviary.)

3

C   *Upper Right-hand.* Solomon, a youthful prince, throned on *R*, makes his mother Bath-sheba sit on the throne with him. Courtiers on each side: two children seated in front. The subject is from 1 Kings ii. 19.

Inscription (second). Totally erased; most likely by Hedgeland.

D   *Lower Right-hand.* The Coronation of the Virgin. She kneels in the centre, full-face. On *L* the Son, seated; on *R* the Father, crowning her. The dove between. Angels playing music in front.

Inscription (lowest). Inserted in 1898. See above under B.

Veni sponsa de libano, veni coronaberis.

Come, O spouse, from Lebanon: come, thou shalt be crowned. (Canticles iv. 8, Vulgate.)

It seems that Hedgeland restored the lower central light of this window. It is known that in 1841 he was allowed to "take down and repair a single central compartment" as an experiment. (Willis and Clark, I. 515.) This, in all likelihood, was the compartment selected.

XXVI.   The West window represents the Last Judgement. It
The West was inserted in 1879 at the expense of the late Francis
window Edmund Stacey, M.A., formerly Fellow. The work was executed by Messrs Clayton and Bell.

In the upper half is Christ as Judge, surrounded by the Apostles and other Saints.

On the lower half in the centre Michael and two other angels with scrolls:

(1) On South:

Judicabit orbem terrae in aequitate et populos in veritate sua.

With righteousness shall He judge the world, and the people with His truth. Ps. xcv. 1.

(2)   On North :

> *Deus in iudicium pro omni errato sive bonum sive malum illud sit.*

> God shall judge every error, whether it be good or evil.
> (Eccl. xii. 14, Vulgate.)

On *L* Angels with the Blessed, among whom is Henry VI. holding a representation of the Chapel.

Scroll : *Venite benedicti patris mei.*

> Come, ye blessed of my Father.   (Matt. xxv. 34.)

On *R* Angels with the Lost.

Scroll : *Discedite a me maledicti.*

> Depart from me, ye cursed.   (Matt. xxv. 41.)

In the Tracery lights are the following coats and devices, in order : Portcullis, Tudor Rose, Shields of King's College, of Eton College, of the University, of King's College, of Henry VI., Henry VII., Henry VIII., Victoria and of Stacey.

Initials of Stacey (F. E. S.).

Shields of the See of Lincoln, impaling Wordsworth (Bp of Lincoln, and then Visitor of the College), and of Okes (then Provost).

Initials H. and R.

APPENDIX.

REMAINS OF PAINTED GLASS IN THE SIDE CHAPELS.

THE following paragraphs are quoted from a paper read by me before the Cambridge Antiquarian Society, and printed in the *Proceedings* of that Society for 1894–98 (xxxvii. pp. 3–12).

The second Chantry from the west on the south side is that of Provost Hacombleyn, who gave the great lectern, was Provost at the time of the glazing of the upper windows, and died in 1538. In the outer window of this Chantry, which gives on the Court, there is glass which has suffered and been mended more than once, and was brought to its present condition by Provost Thackeray. In the tracery lights, are various badges and angels, and on the *right* the four Evangelistic beasts; on the *left* the four Latin Doctors, Ambrose, Jerome, Augustine, and Gregory; Augustine is holding a heart.

In the lower lights are two half-length figures, or rather less than half-lengths. That on the left is Henry VI., who is crowned and holds what I take to be a martyr's crown upon an open book. That on the right is St John the Evangelist.

The character of these two figures is markedly Renaissance, that of the Evangelistic emblems and the four Doctors is equally characteristic of the XVth century. But this is probably merely a case of survival of the older style, or of the using up of glass which the maker had in stock. In the inner window, which gives on the ante-chapel, the original glazing is fairly perfect. The lower lights contain quarries representing lily, rose, pansy, and daisy, and the initials, R. H., both in capitals, and also, R. h., this R being a capital and the h a cursive letter. I suspect that one of these stands for Robertus Hacombleyn, and the other for Rex henricus. In the tracery lights are various devices, of the five wounds, Sun and Moon, etc., and some figures of saints which mark the transition from Gothic work to Renaissance, but partake of the latter character most strongly. They are, counting from the left: St Christopher, St Ursula, Gabriel, the Virgin, St Anne, St John Baptist.

The next Chantry to the east of this is Robert Brassie's, who was Provost in Mary's time from 1556–8 and endowed the Chantry during the brief revival of the old religion. The inner window of this Chantry contains his initials, but little else. In the outer window, however, eight figures have been placed which claim our attention. They are part of a series older by many years than any other glass in the Chapel, being all of them XVth century, and not late in that century, so far as I can judge. Where they originally stood it is impossible to tell. There is a very vague tradition that they came from Ramsey Abbey. I cannot trace this story to its source at present. All that I can definitely say is that the window was restored in November, 1857.

The figures from left to right are—

1. St Peter with keys and an extraordinarily uncouth visage.

2. St Philip with a long cross staff.

3. A Bishop in cope, tunic, dalmatic and alb, with crosier and book. He is beardless, and seems to have a modern head.

4. The Prophet Zephaniah, or Daniel (?), facing right with open book and turban. A scroll: *Accedam ad uos in iudicio et ero* (*testis velox*). The words are from Malachi, but are often given to Daniel or Zephaniah. This figure and the next one to it are plainly portions of a series well known in medieval art. It was very common to depict the Twelve Apostles, each bearing a scroll inscribed with a clause of the Apostles' Creed, and Twelve Prophets, whose scrolls bore quotations from their prophecies corresponding to the portions of the Creed. The text on the scroll we are considering corresponds to the clause " He shall come again to judge both the quick and the dead." The figures of the Apostles in this window, or at least that of St Peter, are too large, I think, to have been originally placed in the same window as Daniel, and neither has any trace of a scroll.

5. King David, seated, with turban and harp. His scroll reads, " *Redemisti me domine deus veritatis*," which corresponds to the clause " was crucified" or else " rose again from the dead," in the Creed.

6. A person whom I take to be a Doctor. He wears a bonnet with gold cord, and fingers a book. His gown has slits in the sleeves, but his arms are not put through the slits. This may be a canonist or writer such as St Yvo of Chartres.

7. A youthful Bishop in mitre, chasuble, and alb, with crosier, round which from top to bottom is wound spirally a very long *vexillum* or handkerchief. I believe this to represent St Erasmus.

8. St James the Great, with scallop on shoulder, long staff and book.

We must now proceed to the northern chantries, passing over two which contain Roger Goad's arms in a most beautiful floral border (1610) and the shield of Matthew Stokys, Esquire Bedell, of Elizabethan time. In the fourth chantry from the east on the north side is a mass of fragments belonging to the series of Apostles and Prophets. The fragments of figures include the top of St Philip's cross staff, and a hand holding a loaf of bread which belonged either to St Simon or St Jude. This detail would of itself almost serve to fix the glass as being of English make, so characteristic of English art is the symbol. On the fragments of scrolls may be deciphered almost the whole of the Apostles' Creed, and many portions of the prophecies corresponding thereto.

In the Chapel, east of this, are the remains of the figure of Hosea, which belonged to the same series, and his scroll is fairly perfect. As to the history of this glass it appears that John Rumpaine, M.A., who entered the college in 1495, glazed one of these windows on the north of the chapel, and I also find two bills of the last century for repairing the vestry windows. These are of 1744, when 49 pieces of coloured glass were put in, and of 1761, when 18 pieces were required. They were also mended in 1647.

Now this glass is too old to be of Rumpaine's giving, and it is my own belief that these large figures must have come from some other church, hardly the old chapel of the College, which was narrow and humble. Possibly the source was Ramsey Abbey, though why glass should have been removed thence before the Dissolution, one cannot guess, and there is no record of a later transfer ; but it is on the whole more likely that they were taken from the Church of St John Zachary, which was demolished in order to make room for the Chapel.

Printed in Great Britain
by Amazon.co.uk, Ltd.,
Marston Gate.